EVESHAM COLLEGE
LIBRARY
920 LAW

The Life of
Stephen Lawrence

By Verna Allette Wilkins
Illustrated by Lynne Willey

Tamarind Ltd

Evesham & Malvern Hills College
Library

22199

Thanks to Mr and Mrs Lawrence, Stuart and Georgina,
Miss Wickes and Mr Gladwell at Eglinton School,
Elvin Udoro, Elizabeth Hawkins and Eddie Burnett

Published by Tamarind Ltd 2001
PO Box 52, Northwood
Middlesex HA6 1UN, UK

Text © Verna Allette Wilkins
Illustrations © Lynne Willey
Cover design © Paula Burgess
Cover photographs – our thanks to Doreen Lawrence
Editor: Simona Sideri

ISBN 1-870516-58-3

All rights reserved.
No part of this publication may be reproduced, stored in a retrieval system,
or transmitted, in any form, or by any means, electrical, mechanical,
photocopying, recording or otherwise without the prior permission
of the publisher.

Printed in Singapore

EVESHAM COLLEGE
LIBRARY
941.085
CLASS NUMBER | 920 LAW
ACCESSION NUMBER | 22199

Peace is not the absence of tension, but the presence of justice. Without justice there will be no peace.

Martin Luther King

Elvin Udoro remembers his best friend Stephen Lawrence.

"I liked Stephen. We had some good times together. He was a great walker. And what a runner! He ran the Greenwich 1988 Mini Marathon to raise money to help children. He was fourteen years old when he did that. He always liked helping people. I remember the time we walked all the way from New Cross to Grove Park. I desperately wanted to get on a bus or a train. But no. Stephen just kept on walking. Fast. I was knocked out with tiredness when we finally arrived. But Stephen wasn't tired. He could have kept going. He could. But that will never happen again. That's all over now..."

Contents

CHAPTER ONE

A life cut short

Stephen Lawrence was born on 13th September, 1974, at the Greenwich District Hospital, in London. His parents were born in Jamaica, in the Caribbean. His father, Neville, emigrated to England in 1960. Stephen's mother, Doreen, arrived two years later, to join her mother in England.

Neville and Doreen met in London in 1970. At that time, Neville worked in a leather factory making clothes and Doreen worked as a bank clerk.

After they married, the Lawrences settled in Plumstead, in south east London. Stephen was their first child.

The Life of Stephen Lawrence

Stephen's parents kept strong ties with family and friends in Jamaica and as soon as all their relatives in England had seen him, Doreen took Stephen to Jamaica to visit his grandmother, Neville's mother.

They spent four wonderful weeks in the sun, and Stephen celebrated his first birthday in Jamaica. It was there that he took his first few steps and immediately tried to run.

Only seventeen years later, Stephen's parents made the same journey, back to Jamaica, this time to bury him.

CHAPTER TWO

A baby brother

Even as a very young child, Stephen loved being with other children. When he was two and a half, his mother took him to join a small playgroup at St Stephen's Church in Woolwich. He settled in happily and went regularly, every Tuesday and every Thursday for a whole year.

One day in April 1977, on the way home from playgroup, Stephen's father said to him, "You have a baby brother! Mum's bringing him home from the hospital tomorrow."

"What's his name?" asked Stephen.

"We'll call him Stuart," replied his father.

Stephen was excited about his new playmate. When his mum

brought Stuart home from the hospital, Stephen gazed at the very small bundle.

"He's very little. He can't play!" said Stephen.

"He'll grow," laughed his father. "You wait and see."

Stephen stayed close to his mother and watched while she fed the baby. At bathtime, Stephen watched him being gently lowered into the small bathtub.

"He's like me. He's a boy baby," Stephen announced and he quickly ran to his bedroom to sort out his precious toy cars and jigsaws to share with baby Stuart.

When Stephen was three and a half his parents decided to move him from his playgroup to the Cyril Henry Nursery in Woolwich.

"Don't want to go there," said Stephen on his first day.

"Why not?" asked his mum.

"Don't want to!" he repeated. He stood outside the door and wouldn't move.

After a few minutes a large group of children arrived. Stephen let go of his mother's hand, said, "Bye, Mum," and trotted into the hall behind them. Within minutes he was in the middle of the group. From that moment, he went happily to nursery every day.

"Can I have crayons today?" was Stephen's favourite question. He loved to draw and paint. If a helper asked him to try something else, he would run over to the sandpit and spend a short time making sand castles and lumpy buildings. After a few minutes, however, he would race right back to his drawing.

At home, baby Stuart was slowly growing bigger, and was beginning to look more like a possible playmate. Stephen was growing up too.

In the mornings, on his way to the nursery, he saw the older boys going to primary school. As the boys walked past, Stephen would shout, "Hello!" but the bigger boys just walked right on.

"When will I go to big school?" he asked his mother most days.

"Soon, love, soon."

"When is soon?" Stephen pestered.

"Not long," his mother answered.

To Stephen it seemed like ages, but eventually the great day arrived. He was four and a half. He was off to big school, Eglinton Primary.

CHAPTER THREE

Starting school

On Stephen's first day at big school, he held his mother's hand down the alley that led from his house to the school. He hopped and skipped all the way, but as soon as they were inside the gate, Stephen raced ahead of his mother and ran, with a huge smile, to Miss Chapple, his new teacher.

Miss Chapple was determined to teach the children in her class to be polite and to have respect for each other and for their teachers. Every morning she made the whole class say together, "Good morning, Miss Chapple. Good morning everybody."

Every morning Stephen's keen voice rang out, "Hello, Miss Chapple. Hello everybody!"

The Life of Stephen Lawrence

"Not 'hello' Stephen, say 'good morning'." She had to work hard to get Stephen to join in her little chorus. But Miss Chapple and Stephen were a good team.

Stephen loved writing time. Sometimes Miss Chapple wrote large letter outlines and the children painted over them to help with their handwriting. Stephen always managed to use loads of paper and then took his work home to his mother. "Some for you, some for Dad and some for Stuart."

Every day, at school, the children were given a drink of milk at eleven o'clock. Many of the children did not like milk.

Miss Chapple had to coax them to take even a few sips. "Come on children. Drink up. Stephen's finished his already!"

Stephen would smile with a milky moustache and was happy to share anyone else's milk if they offered it.

His favourite school lunch was fish fingers and chips. If it was his lucky day, there would be semolina with a blob of jam in the middle, or yellowish sponge pudding with pink custard. At home, his favourite food was Jamaican ackee and saltfish or Caribbean chicken with rice. Stephen loved his mother's cooking.

On Sunday afternoons Neville, Stephen's dad, played Caribbean music and they sat and listened together. Sometimes his dad held his hands and danced around the room with him, showing him some lively steps. Neville loved to dance and was a good dancer.

CHAPTER FOUR

A school trip

Stephen's next teacher at Eglinton Primary was Miss Wickes. "I can picture him now," she remembers. "He didn't like getting things wrong and his work was usually neat. I always had to coax him away from his drawing to get on with his reading and number work. But because his parents shared books with him at home, learning to read was not difficult for him.

"Stephen could sit still and listen, unlike many children his age. At the end of the day, when it was story time, he would always find a seat right at the front.

"He was a great little lad. He didn't deserve to be killed like that. But nobody in the world deserves that. Nobody."

The Life of Stephen Lawrence

Miss Wickes was Stephen's teacher for two years. "He wasn't a goody-two-shoes," she remembers. "He was usually in the middle of the rough and tumble in the playground. He was a brilliant footballer and a popular boy in his group."

Miss Wickes had a couple of very naughty boys in her class. One day, one of them threatened to break Stephen's best pencil. As the boy grabbed for the pencil, Stephen leaped up and gave him a mighty shove. Chairs and tables were knocked over in the squabble.

"You leave me alone, Stephen Lawrence!" the boy shouted.

A teacher came in and found Stephen flat on the floor, in the middle of the commotion. Stephen was blamed for the trouble, and the problem had to be sorted out.

Like everyone, Stephen had his ups and downs. There were times when he clashed with the school bullies. However, it was not long before they all left him alone because he grew much taller than his classmates.

"He was one of the best students in my class," Miss Wickes recalls, smiling. "His parents encouraged him to learn and not mess about, so his school work was excellent. His reading came on in leaps and bounds, but he remained best at art and maths throughout his time at Eglinton School."

The Life of Stephen Lawrence

Miss Wickes was proud of her pupils. One day she decided to reward their good work. There was a buzz of excitement in the class when she told them she was going to take them to visit the Tower of London.

The day arrived and the children were given a delicious packed lunch. They all tumbled onto the coach, pushing and shoving, to get the best seats and to sit near their friends. Just as the coach started on the journey, and even before the school disappeared from sight, the lunch-boxes were opened and the swapping started.

"Give me your cake, and you can have these sandwiches!"

"Do you like apples?"

"Have you got any chocolate?"

"I'll swap you this, for that!" and so it went on. The eating started and soon the lunch-boxes were quite empty.

The morning tour of the Tower was great. They visited the Jewel House to view the Crown Jewels.

"Look here, children," said Miss Wickes. "This is the crown belonging to the Kings and Queens of Great Britain. It has more than 2,800 diamonds, 273 pearls and other gems."

Most of the children were more interested in the grisly contents of the Tower. They gathered around a suit of battle armour that King Henry VIII wore in 1540. Stephen stood next to it and was nearly as tall as the suit of armour made for the fully-grown king.

The Life of Stephen Lawrence

The class walked and walked all around the tower and by late morning they were extraordinarily quiet.

As Stephen and a friend walked along silently, the Beefeater on guard at the Tower remarked, "Are you normally this good? This quiet?"

"Oh yeah," grimaced Stephen, as his stomach let out a thunderous rumble.

They were quiet because they were starving. They'd eaten every bit of their packed lunches by nine fifteen. The next mealtime was at least four hours away.

Stephen's stomach grumbled again. He grimaced and plodded on.

CHAPTER FIVE

Family and friends

In April 1982, when Stephen was seven and a half, his mother had another baby, a beautiful little girl called Georgina. Stephen was delighted.

"She's like a doll!" he said to his mother, and he gently touched his new sister's tiny hands, feet, fingers and toes.

When Georgina began to take her first few steps, she was very unsteady. Stephen stayed close by and grabbed her every time she stumbled. He then lifted her up and held on to her, in case she toppled over.

"Leave her alone, Stephen," begged their mother. "She'll never learn to walk if you carry her everywhere. She won't get hurt."

The Life of Stephen Lawrence

As Stephen, Stuart and Georgina grew up, they took part in many different activities. Their parents encouraged them to do things they enjoyed. Mum and Dad were always on hand to drop them off and fetch them, and took an interest in all the children's hobbies.

The boys joined the Plumstead Cubs and went canoeing, swimming, rambling and camping. Their rambles sometimes took them into Shrewsbury Park, but more often deep into Oxleas Wood, an ancient forest with huge old trees. These day trips were great fun, but the real excitement was Cub camp!

Stephen's mother remembers one Cub camp very well. Stephen was extremely excited about camping in the woods for a week. Five days before leaving, he had already packed one cup, one plate, a tea towel and a torch in his rucksack.

"What's the torch for, Stephen?" asked Doreen.

"That's for if we have to go to the toilet at night, Mum. It may not be near the tent."

"That could be interesting!" giggled his mother.

Finally the morning came when the Cubs were leaving.

As she waved him off, his mother said, "Take care, while you're away, son. And, by the way, I put a toothbrush, soap and a towel in your bag."

"Thanks, Mum," called Stephen as he went off with his friends.

A week later, Stephen arrived back bursting with news.

The Life of Stephen Lawrence

"We collected wood for fires and cooked in the open. We put up the tent ourselves and..." Stephen let out an enormous sneeze.

His parents burst out laughing.

Stephen was absolutely filthy. His face and hands were encrusted and grubby. He had grey bits in his hair. "It was great, Mum!" said Stephen as he followed her to the bathroom. The toothbrush, soap and towel were still in his bag, exactly how his mother had packed them.

When Stephen was nine he started going to Sunday School at Burnage Road Methodist Church. It was here that he met Elvin Udoro, who remained his lifelong and closest friend. The boys saw each other every week and when the church arranged trips, picnics and Christmas parties the two of them teamed up.

Once when Father Christmas came, Stephen was sitting between Elvin and his mum.

He whispered loudly, "That's not Father Christmas!"

"Yes it is!" whispered Elvin.

"No, it can't be. He's wearing trainers. Father Christmas wears boots," argued Stephen.

Mum whispered back, "Never mind his feet, he has presents for you two."

The boys stopped talking immediately.

CHAPTER SIX

School and sports

In September 1982, when he was eight years old, Stephen moved up to Eglinton Junior School. It was built on an enormous corner site and the building was already over one hundred years old when Stephen went there. When the school was first built, there were only a few houses around it, but as the years went by, large housing estates sprouted all around, and the school filled with the children from those houses.

The staff at Eglinton organised many activities, and for Stephen, the highlight of one summer was a field trip to Swanage.

He raced home from school with the letter, calling out, "Can I go? Can I go?" as soon as he saw his mother.

The Life of Stephen Lawrence

Stephen never forgot that week. It stayed hot and he had lots of fun. He talked about the donkey rides on the beach for weeks.

Stephen was becoming more and more interested in sports. His mother had to encourage and sometimes pester him to get his homework done. "How come I never have to remind you to go running or swimming?" she asked.

Stephen was one of the first in his group to get a silver swimming medal. He was also a seriously fast runner and everyone wanted him on their team. Sports day was always exciting for Stephen.

The children went in the large, blue, school coach to the playing fields in Shrewsbury Park at the top of Shooters Hill. From there, they could see a large part of London spread out before them.

Stephen won many races in Shrewsbury Park. One race that he was particularly good at made the teachers laugh out loud and the children scream. It was the 'late for school' race. Articles of clothing were placed along the track and the children raced to the finishing line, stopping five times to pile on sets of clothing.

As Stephen piled on clothes at high speed and flew along the track, his classmates shouted, "Go, Stephen! Go!"

Some runners collapsed in a tangle of clothes a long way from the end. Stephen arrived at the finishing line first. He was hot, tired and looked enormous, in several layers of clothes.

The Life of Stephen Lawrence

Afterwards, he sat quietly to rest and get his energy back for the 100 metres sprint, his special race. He won it every time.

Life was very busy for everyone in the Lawrence family at this time. Doreen and Neville had the three children to look after and as they grew older, Stephen, Stuart and Georgina had many friends and more and more activities to go to.

There were always jobs to be done at home too. Stephen was happy to keep an eye on Stuart and Georgina when his parents were busy around the house or garden, but he preferred those jobs that took him on the road. Sometimes, he helped with bits of shopping and he was also allowed to go to the library on his own to change his books. It was a short bus ride away, and Stephen would scamper out of the house, full of confidence and unafraid.

At Junior school, Stephen was a good pupil. "I know that some people are uncomfortable with speaking about the dead and try to paint them in an unrealistic, saintly light. I don't have to do that with Stephen," said Mr Gladwell, his Junior school teacher. "Stephen wanted to learn. He was good at most subjects and brilliant at sports. He had a few weak spots, like most of us, but everyone could see clearly how good he was in Maths and Art – especially drawing.

The Life of Stephen Lawrence

"I taught Stephen for two years in all. One episode springs to mind… Stephen could be really stubborn and so could I. One day, quite out of character, he handed in some awful, shoddy work. I knew from past experience that he could do one hundred percent better.

"'Go and do this properly, Stephen,' I said.

"Stephen stood staring at the awful piece of work.

"'Did you hear me?' I said.

"Stephen didn't budge.

"'If you don't take this away and do it properly, I shall tear it up.' I threatened.

"Stephen still didn't budge.

"At this point, I was aware that I should not have made that threat. I was wrong, but I thought I had to be consistent. I didn't want to lose face, so I tore up his work.

"I never expected Stephen to stand up to me. We were both wrong. Stephen went home angry and upset.

"Doreen, his mother, was working at the school at that time. She came to see me and we sorted it out together. I apologised. Stephen did too. We agreed that we had both made a bit of a mess of things.

"Stephen was a good lad. We must make sure that we help all our children learn to live in peace. What happened to Stephen must never happen again."

CHAPTER SEVEN

Secondary school

Stephen's years at Eglinton Juniors passed quickly and in 1986, when he was nearly twelve he went to Blackheath Bluecoats Secondary School. Now he was at school with his friend Elvin. At Bluecoats, Stephen could start to concentrate on the subjects he really enjoyed.

One of his real strengths was still life drawing and Elvin was great at painting. Stephen was also good at Maths. So, he helped Elvin with Maths and drawing while Elvin helped him with colour work.

The two young, enthusiastic friends earned a little money drawing and painting the pupils at their school. Some of their

The Life of Stephen Lawrence

schoolmates wanted portraits of themselves wearing their favourite trainers or track suits. The lads did many portraits of self-conscious smilers and scowlers, holding cricket bats or showing off magnificent trainers.

"He was so active. Always on the move. My best friend. It was Stephen's brilliant record on the running track that influenced me to start running. He made it seem so easy!" remembers Elvin. "I wasn't bad at running, but I could never match Stephen's speed. I miss him."

Stephen's younger sister Georgina was very close to him too. She remembers, "He used to collect me from Primary School when Mum was busy. He was always there. He never forgot. His turn to collect me was on a Wednesday.

"We had cookery that day. Everyone in the class was allowed to have four peppermint creams. I would eat two and save two for Stephen when he came to pick me up.

"Sometimes they were soggy and squashed flat. But Stephen always said, 'Thanks Georgie! Lovely!' and gobbled them up.

"At home, I sometimes used to sneak into the bedroom that Stephen and Stuart shared. There were loads of really interesting things in there. Tapes, CDs, comics and posters. Stephen also had a really good pair of binoculars that he thought were special. I used to pick them up and stand at the window staring out for ages.

"One day, I was concentrating so hard watching a couple way up the street, I didn't hear Stephen come into the room. All I heard was 'Georgina... what!'

"I dropped the binoculars. They crashed to the floor. I ducked past him, ran into my room and hid for ages. He was really mad at me. It took quite a long time before he let me back into the room to listen to some of his great music. He loved me. He's still here with us in spirit, you know!"

CHAPTER EIGHT

Helping others

In 1988, Stephen signed up for the Greenwich Mini Marathon, sponsored by Mars – the chocolate people. Before the race, Stephen pestered family, friends and neighbours to sponsor him. He managed to get a long list of sponsors and the money he collected went to Great Ormond Street Hospital for Sick Children.

"Stephen was like that," remembers Neville, his father. "He took part in the marathon because he loved helping people. He was so full of life… I remember listening to music with him. I remember dancing with him when he was very little… I will not dance until Stephen's killers have been brought to justice! I haven't danced for years. I would really love to dance again."

The Life of Stephen Lawrence

Two weeks before the Mini Marathon, Capital Radio arranged a huge party in Jubilee Gardens, Westminster, to support the enormous effort by those wonderful children working to help other children. There was food and drink, fantastic activities and lots of fun. There was an enormous buzz in the air.

In one of the games, Stephen had to turn his team mate into an Egyptian mummy with yards and yards of toilet paper.

"Don't wrap too tight around the nose, Stephen," mumbled the mummy, as Stephen wrapped toilet paper round his head. The crowd cheered with delight as the mummy strutted around straight-legged, followed by a laughing Stephen trying to tuck in stray banners of tissue.

The highlight of the party was the arrival of Stephen's heroes, two of the most famous sporting celebrities of that time: Linford Christie, the 100 metres world champion and Tessa Sanderson, the Olympic javelin thrower. It was a great day.

Two weeks later, Stephen successfully completed the Mini Marathon and collected the sponsorship money for Great Ormond Street Hospital.

Then one day, not long after the marathon, Stephen himself ended up in hospital.

He'd arrived at school early one Wednesday morning and joined

The Life of Stephen Lawrence

in a football game in the playground. Seconds before the bell, he made a daring tackle, pitched forward, fell and broke his left wrist.

At the time, his mum had gone back to college. She was in a lecture when she heard her name called. "Mrs Lawrence, there's a call for you in the office…"

It was Stephen's school phoning to say that Stephen had been taken to Brookes Hospital in Shooters Hill. She raced over there.

When she arrived she went straight in to see him and gave him a big hug. "Are you all right son?"

"Ouch!" said Stephen. "It hurts and it's swelling, look!"

They had to wait for a long time in the Accident and Emergency Department.

The doctor who examined Stephen was very kind. "I think you have broken a bone in here!" he said gently, prodding Stephen's arm. "I'll send you to the x-ray department. It won't hurt."

The x-rays showed up the fracture and Stephen's arm was put into plaster. The doctor also did a blood test and discovered that Stephen had the sickle cell trait.

Sickle cell is a blood disorder that is passed down through families. The red blood cells contain sickle haemoglobin, which makes them become curved (or shaped like a sickle). Because of their shape, sickle cells can become stuck in small blood vessels forming plugs. This can stop the blood flow and may cause damage to the tissue.

"Does that mean I'm sick, Mum?" he asked when the results came.

"No, son, you're lucky, you don't have the illness. You have the sickle cell trait. It runs in your dad's family."

"So what can happen then, Mum?"

"It just means that when you grow up and want to have babies it would be wise to check your partner. If she has the trait too, the children could have sickle cell disorder. But let's just get this arm better for now, love. Don't worry!"

CHAPTER NINE

One of the boys

Stuart remembers joining his older brother at Blackheath Bluecoats School. "It was great having a big brother. No one messed with me. Stephen was tall and cool and had loads of friends. It sometimes worked against me, though. I was a bit of a tearaway, and Stephen had a good reputation. He was a good worker. Every time I did something wrong, the teachers at Bluecoats kept repeating, 'Not a bit like your brother, are you!' It was annoying, but Stephen and I stayed close. We ran together for the Cambridge Harriers. He encouraged me to stick with it when I wanted to give up.

"There were times though, when he wanted to go out with his

The Life of Stephen Lawrence

mates. He didn't want a little brother trailing him. 'Go on Stuart, go with your own friends!' he would say, but that never stopped me. I'd just hang around until he let me join in with his group."

The Lawrence children had many cousins but most of them were Stephen's age and older. Stuart was out on a limb. At one particular family gathering, Stuart, as usual, was trying to get in with the older ones. They were playing a new, very fast and exciting computer game.

"Can I have a go?" Stuart begged.

They all ignored him. He sat around for ages, being absolutely miserable, until Stephen felt sorry for him

"Come on fellas. Give bruv a break. Let him have a go," Stephen begged. Finally, they gave him a turn.

Stuart took the controls, got stuck in and beat them all. The older boys were shocked at his speed and technique and thought this was hilarious!

"I was so excited," Stuart remembers. "I jumped in the air, hit Stephen on the shoulder, and hurt my hand. Stephen just grinned.

"What wasn't so hilarious though was when Stephen wanted to wear a particular shirt, only to find that I'd borrowed it. What really got him going, though, was when I borrowed tapes and CDs and didn't return them. That was when the real ructions happened.

The Life of Stephen Lawrence

"Stephen's death has had a huge effect on me," says Stuart. "I've changed ever so much. I believe that I'm more careful and caring. You don't expect your brother to die like that! I miss him. I take each day as it comes. I want to look after my sister and my mum and dad. I want them all to be proud of me. We have all suffered so much."

CHAPTER TEN

Music and work

Both Stephen and Elvin liked listening to music. Stephen loved Soul and Hip Hop. The two friends listened for hours to Leaders of the New School which was Stephen's favourite group. He also liked Tupac Shakur, Ice Cube and Public Enemy.

His teenage years were a magical time for Stephen. He was young and carefree. His music idols were big and loud. The music was great and by the time he turned sixteen, he could earn just enough money helping his father with a painting and decorating business in Marylebone and doing a Saturday job.

Nearly every penny of his earnings went to buy tapes. But he couldn't afford to buy tickets to go to see his favourite bands live.

The Life of Stephen Lawrence

Then, one day, he got lucky. Stephen was with a school friend called Jermayne.

"Come on Jermayne, listen to this competition." Stephen turned up his radio to full volume. "We could win this. All we have to do is name all the tracks on the latest Public Enemy album. I know most of them."

"So do I," said Jermayne and the two gave each other a wild high five. They phoned in to the station and they won! The prize was three tickets to the Public Enemy concert.

"Thanks. Yesssssss!!!" said Elvin when Stephen gave him a free ticket.

"Forget it, son! This is rubbish. You're going nowhere," said Elvin's mother, and she confiscated his ticket. She didn't approve of the band or any of the modern music the boys liked.

Elvin was devastated. Stephen and Jermayne went to the concert. It was a roaring success.

Soon afterwards Stephen and Elvin hatched a money-making scheme.

"I know where we can buy some low priced T-shirts," Stephen told Elvin one day. "We could buy some and paint them."

"That would be great," agreed Elvin. "We could paint faces of bands and famous people on them and sell them."

The Life of Stephen Lawrence

Their business idea went down well. They had many requests for the heads of Malcolm X and also many famous rappers of the time. Most popular were Public Enemy faces. It wasn't long before they were painting portraits of famous people on all sorts of things – caps, exercise book covers, jackets and of course, T-shirts.

Around this time, a TV programme, *The Word*, was running on Channel 4. One lucky evening, Stephen and Elvin managed to get into the TV studios to see a live show starring Public Enemy. It was brilliant and they were doubly excited because they were carrying a present for a member of the band.

At the end of the show, they were allowed to present Flavour Flav, their favourite rapper, with a stunningly painted boiler suit with his own face painted on the front, back and arms.

He was delighted with the gift. "Thanks guys, thanks so much! I'll cherish this," said the star with a huge grin and two high fives.

Having met some famous people, Stephen and Elvin developed a taste for the bright lights.

"Hey guys! Guess what?" Stephen announced to his friends one day. "Denzel Washington's coming to England to make a film. And they're looking for extras!"

"Denzel who?" asked Stuart.

"Y'know, the black Hollywood superstar," explained Elvin. "The one women go crazy over. He starred in *Much Ado About*

The Life of Stephen Lawrence

Nothing. He was a prince. We've got to get on set, Stephen, we've just got to."

Denzel was in London to play a Falklands War soldier in *For Queen and Country* and Stephen and Elvin managed to get work as extras. All they had to do was mingle with loads of other people in the background while the cameras rolled and the stars performed. They loved it. They were unpaid, but it was a wonderful experience.

They kept in touch with fame by getting Saturday jobs in a shop in Camden Town where all the big stars went to order their tour T-shirts. It was so exciting when really famous people and even not so famous people came in.

One Saturday, just before closing time, Busta Rhymes and Salt 'n' Peppa came in. The young assistants queued up to serve them.

The great thing about working at the shop was that it helped Stephen and Elvin get into concerts free. This was a great bonus because the wages at the shop were extremely low.

Despite all this activity in the music world, Stephen continued working hard at school.

CHAPTER ELEVEN

Further education

As the children grew older Doreen decided to work towards her university degree. During their early years, she had little time to herself. She looked after the children and the home and did a job as well. She had gone to college and passed the exams she needed, so now she could start university.

"I'm going to be very busy studying and looking after all of you," she announced one day. "I'll make a rota. If we all help, then nobody will collapse under the strain."

Everyone in the family had a job to do. From shopping, to house cleaning, washing up and cooking. It worked fairly well, most of the time.

The Life of Stephen Lawrence

Then came Christmas and it was the Lawrences' turn to feed family and friends. The house was full of people, masses of food had to be cooked, and tons of washing up needed to be done. Everyone had to lend a hand.

It was Stephen's name on the list to do the washing up after the huge meal. He stuck with it. The stack of dishes took him more than two and a half hours to clear. But with his favourite tracks playing on his headphones, he carried on and on.

Life at home, with his parents, brother and sister, rolled on. In 1991 Stephen took his GCSE examinations. He was keen to get the right grades in order to go to university to study architecture. The following year, his school arranged for him to do work experience with a firm of architects in Southwark, in south east London.

The firm, Timothy Associates, used Stephen on their inner city regeneration projects in Deptford and Lewisham.

Arthur Timothy explained Stephen's role with the company. "He worked on the drawings for one project involving forty flats, twelve workshops and the landscaping around the area. Stephen was a good lad with a brilliant future. He was keen and reliable. He could have been a great benefit to this country."

Stephen worked in the office and continued with his athletics. He had a hectic social life but always made time for family.

CHAPTER TWELVE

A tragic end

At 10.30 p.m. on 22nd April 1993, Stephen and a friend, Duwayne Brooks, were on their way home from Stephen's uncle's house. They had spent the evening watching TV and playing computer games.

When the eighteen year olds reached Well Hall Road, in Eltham, they decided to catch a bus. While Duwayne waited at the bus stop, Stephen went to see if a bus was coming. He walked a short distance towards Dickson Road to get a better look.

Duwayne called out to ask him if he could see a bus. Instead of Stephen's reply, Dwayne heard voices shouting nasty racist abuse. He swung around and in a split second, saw a group of five or six white youths racing furiously towards Stephen. Duwayne ran and screamed for Stephen to run with him.

The gang surrounded Stephen, attacked him and then escaped down Dickson Road.

That hellish attack lasted only a few grim seconds.

Mr and Mrs Conor Taaffe had been to a prayer meeting at a nearby church. As they were walking towards Well Hall roundabout, they saw Stephen and Duwayne running towards them.

"Stephen was holding his upper chest with one hand," said Mr Taaffe. Almost immediately, he saw Stephen crash onto the pavement. "Duwayne was standing in the middle of the road trying to flag down passing cars. They drove straight past. He then ran into a nearby telephone box."

Mr and Mrs Taaffe stayed with Stephen. When the ambulance arrived, they went back to the church to pray for him.

Stephen died from the stab wounds. He was stabbed to a depth of about five inches on both sides of the front of his body and arm. He bled heavily. The stabs cut through the main blood vessels to his heart.

Dr Shepherd, the pathologist who examined his body, said "It's surprising that he managed to get 130 yards with all the injuries he had, and also the fact that one deep and penetrating cut had caused the collapse of his right lung. It is due to Stephen's physical fitness that he was able to run the distance he did before collapsing."

Stephen Lawrence was brutally killed on 22nd April, 1993. To date, nobody has been convicted of this awful crime.

Stephen was not involved in any criminal activity. He died a victim of an unprovoked racist attack.

Stephen did not know his killers, and his killers did not know him.

To date, no-one has been put into prison for committing this terrible crime. The police continue their work.

At the request of Mr and Mrs Lawrence, Stephen's parents, an Inquiry was set up by the Right Honourable Jack Straw MP, the Home Secretary, in July 1997. The Report on the Inquiry was by Sir William Macpherson of Cluny, advised by Tom Cook, the Right Reverend Dr John Sentamu and Dr Richard Stone. They reported that "Neville and Doreen Lawrence have together been the mainspring of this inquiry... their dignity and courtesy have been an example to all..."

The Inquiry recommended that, "Consideration be given to amendment of the National Curriculum aimed at valuing cultural diversity and preventing racism, in order better to reflect the needs of a diverse society."

The Stephen Lawrence Charitable Trust, 48 New Cavendish Street, London W1G 8TG. Tel: 020 7486 2066

Stephen Lawrence Family Campaign information is available on the internet at:
www.blink.org.uk/campaign/stevelaw/slmain.htm

More information is available on the internet at:
www.official-documents.co.uk/document/cm42/4262/4262.htm